A Child's Day In ...

My Life in
FRANCE

Patience Coster

W
FRANKLIN WATTS
LONDON • SYDNEY

First published in 2015 by Franklin Watts

Copyright © Arcturus Holdings Limited

Franklin Watts
338 Euston Road
London
NW1 3BH

Franklin Watts Australia
Level 17/207 Kent Street, Sydney, NSW 2000

Produced by Arcturus Publishing Limited,
26/27 Bickels Yard, 151–153 Bermondsey Street, London SE1 3HA

Editor: Joe Harris
Designer: Ian Winton

Picture credits:
All photography courtesy of Alain Pitton/Demotix/Corbis

A CIP catalogue record for this book is available from the British Library.

Dewey Decimal Classification Number: 944'.08412

ISBN: 978 1 4451 3737 7

Franklin Watts is a division of Hachette Children's Books, an Hachette UK company.
www.hachette.co.uk

Printed in China

SL004298UK

Supplier 03, Date 1014, Print Run 3567

Contents

My day begins 4

Going to school 6

Registration 8

Morning classes 10

Maths lesson 12

Lunchtime 14

Back to school 16

Afternoon classes 18

Homework 20

Baking a cake 22

Music practice 24

Playtime 26

Dinner and bedtime 28

Glossary 30

Further information 31

Index 32

My day begins

Salut! My name is Louise. I am ten years old. I live with my mum, dad and little sister Corinne in Damazan, a village in south-west France.

There are around 1,300 people in Damazan. My family lives in an old farmhouse on the edge of the village.

Louise says ...

We have bread, yoghurt and hot chocolate for breakfast.

Corinne is drinking hot chocolate from her bowl.

When breakfast is finished, I brush my hair and tie it back for school.

My country

France is a large country in Western Europe. It has a population of around 66 million people. Damazan is in the Lot-et-Garonne region. It is a beautiful, hilly part of France named after the Lot and Garonne rivers.

8.00 AM

Going to school

Corinne and **I** go to the *école élémentaire* or primary school. The school takes both boys and girls and there is no uniform so we can wear our normal clothes.

We study French, maths, geography, history, art and a foreign language. **I** am learning English.

Louise says...

My school is just down the road in the village so I walk there most days.

On the way to school I meet my friend Nicole. We have known each other since we were little.

Speaking French

Here in France, we speak French. French is an important language in many other countries, including Switzerland, Belgium, Canada and many African countries.

Registration

My school is called Groupe Scolaire de Damazan. State schools in France are secular. This means there is no religious teaching or morning worship.

Louise says ...

Before school some of us get together to rehearse for the end of year show.

To start the day, instead of assembly, we have registration. We each have to answer 'Oui' – meaning 'Yes' – when our name is called.

Types of school

In France, children start primary school at the age of six. We go on to *collège* or middle school at age 11. From the age of 15 we go to *lycée* or high school. There are two main types of *lycée* – general and technical.

Morning classes

I am in class **CM1**. We are getting ready to go to middle school, so we do lots of tests.

There are 18 students in my class. We have to work quietly during lesson time.

I memorise some language rules about verbs.

Louise says ...

I practise writing phrases in my notebook.

Education

There are five classes in primary school – CP, CE1, CE2, CM1 and CM2. CP is preparatory class, CE is elementary class and CM is middle class. The last two classes prepare students for middle school.

Maths lesson

After breaktime, which lasts 15 minutes, we have a maths test. We are working on addition, division, multiplication and subtraction.

I finish the test quickly so I'm allowed to read a book.

Louise says ...

Maths is my favourite subject.

Afterwards our teacher, Madame Girard, gives us a *défi mathémathique* – a maths challenge. We work in teams of three. The first group to finish with the right answers gets a reward.

The importance of maths

The French emperor Napoleon Bonaparte believed that maths would make France a successful nation. Today, many French people still say that maths is the most important subject in school. Many famous mathematicians are French.

Lunchtime

We have a two-hour break for lunch. Today Corinne is staying at school to eat in the canteen. I walk home on my own.

I wash my hands while Mum makes lunch. I'm really hungry after working so hard!

14

Louise says ... Mmm, this croque-monsieur is delicious!

A croque-monsieur is a grilled ham and cheese sandwich.

French food

The French diet consists mainly of fresh vegetables, meat and cheeses. French people eat their main meal in the evening, with often just a sandwich or quiche for lunch. Famous dishes include onion soup and thin pancakes called *crêpes*.

Back to school

After lunch, **I** walk back to school so that **I** arrive half an hour before class starts.

Louise says ...

I like going home for lunch, but I want to make sure I spend some time with my friends as well.

We play the sparrowhawk game then rehearse some more for the school show.

It's time to start lessons again, so we go back to the classroom.

Sparrowhawk game

For the sparrowhawk game, one child is the hawk and stands in the middle of the playground. When the hawk calls out 'I'm coming!' the other children run across the playground. If the hawk catches them, they become sparrowhawks too.

Afternoon classes

In the afternoon we have geography. We are learning about the different landscape features of France.

Louise says ...

If there is anything we don't understand, Madame Girard explains it to us.

Then we have a French grammar lesson. Grammar is the correct way of speaking and writing. In France we think this is very important. Today we are learning about punctuation.

I get up to answer some questions in front of the class, using the interactive whiteboard.

Mont Blanc

The biggest mountain in Europe is in the French Alps on the Italian border. Called Mont Blanc (French for 'White Mountain'), it is **4,810 m (15,781 ft)** high. A 11-km- (7-mile-) long tunnel through the mountain connects France with Italy.

Homework

School is finished for the day – but I still have an hour of homework to do. We work hard in France!

Louise says ...

I meet up with Corinne and we walk home together.

I eat some baguette with cherry jam before starting on my homework.

Tomorrow I have tests in geography and history. My mum helps me to revise.

The French Revolution

The most famous event in French history is the French Revolution. In 1789, the ordinary people rose up against the richest people in the country. They removed the monarchy (the king and his family) from power. Many people who disagreed with the revolution were put to death with a machine called the guillotine.

Baking a cake

Hurrah – now for some down time! I love baking, so today I'm going to make a salted caramel cake.

FLOUR

I need eggs, butter, flour and sugar to start.

Corinne comes to help. We need to blend all the ingredients together until the mixture is soft and creamy.

Pâtisseries

A *pâtisserie* is a bakery that specializes in making fancy pastries and sweets. There is a *pâtisserie* in almost every town in France. French pastry chefs train for a long time. This shows in the quality of their cakes, which are often works of art to look at as well as delicious to eat!

6.00 PM

Music practice

While the cake is baking I do some music practice. I am learning to play the oboe.

I have lessons at a music school in Tonneins, a nearby town.

Louise says ...

Learning how to blow into the mouthpiece of the oboe is quite tricky.

When I've finished practising I send some messages to my friends online.

Music in France

Many famous composers (writers of music) come from France. People all over the world love the music of Hector Berlioz, Maurice Ravel and Claude Debussy. *Chanson française*, a style of solo singing with a very long history, is still popular in France. Great artists include Edith Piaf, Juliette Greco, Charles Aznavour and Jacques Brel.

Playtime

Before dinner, we go outside to play. We are lucky to have a big garden and to live in the countryside. There are lots of trees, places to play and fresh air.

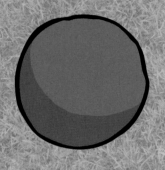

Corinne and I play a game of catch. The most popular sport in France is football.

We are eating outside this evening, so I bring out the salted caramel cake we have made.

Then we shower and get changed into our pyjamas.

Boules

A game called *boules* is very popular all over France. It is played with heavy metal balls on sandy ground. The goal is to throw or roll your ball as close as possible to a small ball, which is the target.

Dinner and bedtime

For dinner we have omelette and salad, with melon for pudding. We save the cake for last – everyone loves it!

Louise says ...

I like omelette, but I don't like salad so much!

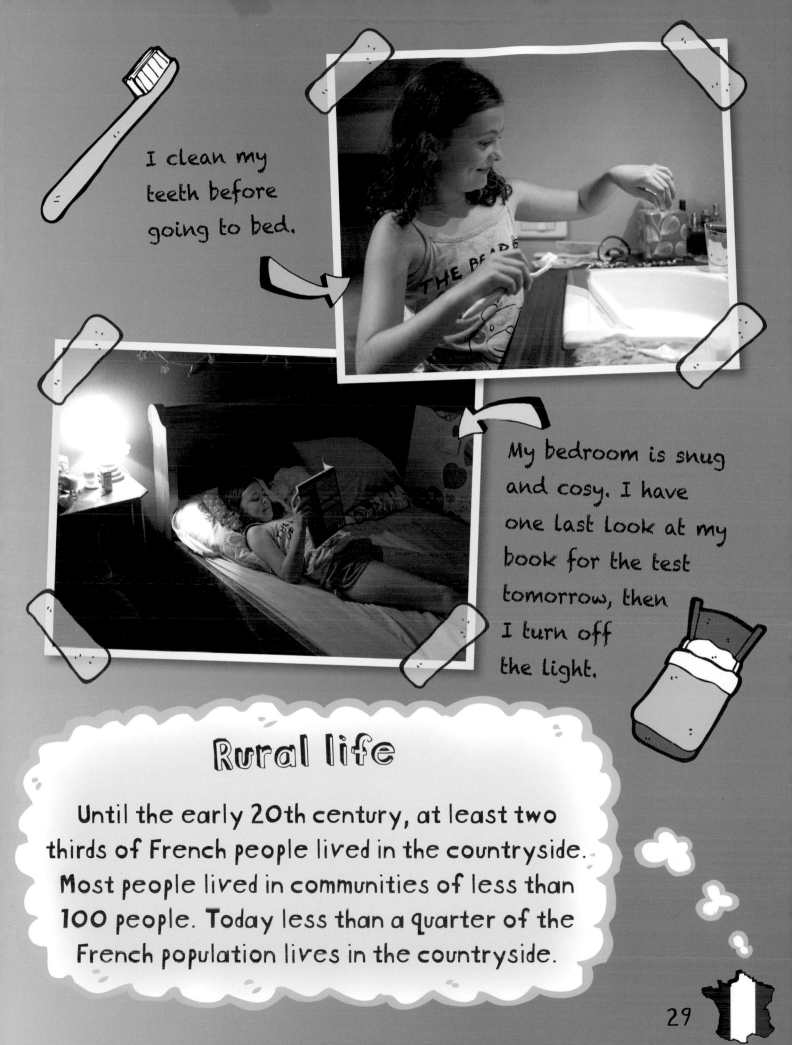

I clean my teeth before going to bed.

My bedroom is snug and cosy. I have one last look at my book for the test tomorrow, then I turn off the light.

Rural life

Until the early 20th century, at least two thirds of French people lived in the countryside. Most people lived in communities of less than 100 people. Today less than a quarter of the French population lives in the countryside.

Glossary

Alps A European mountain range stretching across the countries of France, Switzerland, Italy, Austria, Slovenia and Germany.

baguette A long, thin loaf of bread, usually white, with a crunchy crust.

communities Groups of people living together in the same place.

crêpes Thin pancakes usually served smeared with jam or filled with a savoury, creamy sauce.

croque monsieur A cheese and ham sandwich, served hot (fried or grilled).

elementary Introductory or basic.

grammar The rules and structure of a language.

guillotine A machine with a heavy blade, designed to drop suddenly, used for beheading people.

lycée A French secondary school.

monarchy A system of government which has a king or queen as head of state.

omelette A dish of beaten eggs fried in a frying pan, often served with a savoury filling of cheese or mushrooms.

population The total number of people living in a place, such as a country.

preparatory A school for very young children which prepares them for elementary school.

punctuation Marks in writing, for example, comma, full stop and semi-colon, used to separate sentences and make meaning clear.

quiche A savoury tart with a filling made of egg custard, often flavoured with vegetables, cheese and/or ham.

secular Not religious.

verbs Words used to describe actions, such as run, walk, swim, etc.

Further information

Websites

kids.nationalgeographic.com/explore/countries/france.html
  Geography, nature, people, culture, government, economy and history.

www.bbc.co.uk/learningzone/clips/daily-school-routines-in-french
  Video clip featuring Papo the parrot, who learns what life is like at a school in France.

http://dinolingo.com/blog/2011/05/04/french-culture/
  Fun facts for kids — food, music, language and more . . .

www.discoverfrance.net/
  Culture, history, language, travel and more . . .

www.kids-world-travel-guide.com/france-facts.html
  Facts researched by and for children.

Further reading

Been There! France by Annabel Savery (Franklin Watts, 2014)

Countries: France by Ruth Thomson (Wayland, 2013)

Cultural Traditions in France by Lynn Peppas (Crabtree Publishing Company, 2014)

France: A Benjamin Blog and His Inquisitive Dog Guide by Anita Ganeri, (Raintree, 2014)

Looking at Countries: France by Jillian Powell (Franklin Watts, 2010)

Young Reporter in France series by Sue Finnie and Daniele Bourdais (Franklin Watts, 2014)

Index

Africa 7
Alps 19
art 6
assembly 9

baking 22-23
Belgium 7
boules 27
bread 4
break time 12
breakfast 4-5

Canada 7
cheeses 15
class size 10
classes 10-11, 18-19
collège 9
composers 25
crêpes 15
croque-monsieur 15

Damazan 4, 5
dinner 28

école élémentaire 6
education 11
English 6
Europe 5

food 4, 14-15, 21, 22,
    23, 28
France 4, 5, 7,13

French language 7
French Revolution 21

games 17, 26, 27
geography 6, 18, 19, 21
grammar 19
guillotine 21

high school 9
history 6, 21
homework 20-21
hot chocolate 4, 5

language 7, 11
lessons 10-11, 12-13,
    18-19
Lot-et-Garonne region
    5
lunch 14-15
lycée 9

mathematicians 13
maths 6, 12-13
middle class 11
middle school 9, 11
Mont Blanc 19
music 24-25

Napoleon Bonaparte 13

omelettes 28
onion soup 15

pâtisserie 23
playtime 26-27
population 4, 5
preparatory class 11
primary school 6, 9, 11

quiche 15

registration 9
religion 8
rural life 29

school 5, 6-7, 8-9,
    10-11, 12-13, 16-17,
    18-19
school age 9
singers 25
sparrowhawk game 17
state schools 8
Switzerland 7

tests 10, 12, 21, 29

uniform 4

Series contents

My Life in BRAZIL

• Waking up • Getting dressed • Walking to school • Lessons begin
• Break time • Back to work! • Lunchtime • More lessons • School's
out • Helping at home • Downtime • Hobbies • Dinner and bedtime

My Life in FRANCE

• My day begins • Going to school • Registration • Morning classes
• Maths lesson • Lunchtime • Back to school • Afternoon classes
• Homework • Baking a cake • Music practice • Playtime
• Dinner and bedtime

My Life in INDIA

• Morning • Getting ready • Going to school • School assembly
• Lessons • Art and music • Sport • Hometime • Lunch • Out and about
• Shopping • At home • Evening meal

My Life in INDONESIA

• Morning • Breakfast • Walking to school • Morning register • Lesson
time • Physical education • Playtime and lunch • Traditional dancing
• Hometime • Music practice • Family shop • At home • Evening meal

My Life in JAMAICA

• My home • Breakfast • Time to go • The school bus • My school
• Lessons begin • Break time • Maths class • Lunchtime • Afternoon
lessons • Dance class • Shopping • Dinner and bedtime

My Life in KENYA

• Getting up • Breakfast • Walking to school • Lesson time • Playtime
• In the library • Eating lunch • Afternoon lessons • Walking home
• Fetching water • At the market • Evening meal • Going to bed